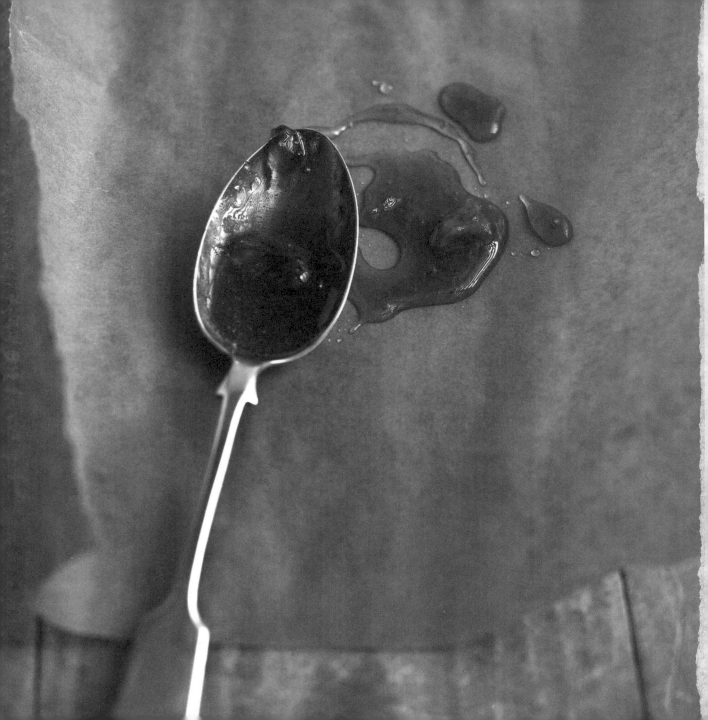

The Women's Institute

homemade
jams and chutneys

SIMON &
SCHUSTER
ILLUSTRATED

London · New York · Sydney · Toronto · New Delhi
A CBS COMPANY

the **WI**
INSPIRING WOMEN

Midge Thomas

First published in Great Britain
by Simon & Schuster UK Ltd, 2012
A CBS Company

Simon & Schuster Illustrated Books
Simon & Schuster UK Ltd
222 Gray's Inn Road, London WC1X 8HB

www.simonandschuster.co.uk

Simon & Schuster Australia, Sydney
Simon & Schuster India, New Delhi

1 3 5 7 9 10 8 6 4 2

Editorial Director: **Francine Lawrence**
Senior Commissioning Editor: **Nicky Hill**
Project Editor: **Nicki Lampon**
Designer: **Richard Proctor**
Food Photographer: **William Shaw**
Stylist and Art Direction: **Tony Hutchinson**
Home Economist: **Sara Lewis**
Commercial Director: **Ami Richards**

Colour reproduction by Dot Gradations Ltd, UK
Printed and bound in China

A CIP catalogue for this book is
available from the British Library.

978-0-85720-858-3

Recipes in this book were first published in 2002
under the title *Best-kept Secrets of the Women's
Institute: Jams, Pickles & Chutneys.*

With thanks to www.jamjarshop.com

Notes on the recipes

Both metric and imperial measurements have been
given in all recipes. Use one set of measurements
only and not a mixture of both. Spoon measures are
level and 1 tablespoon = 15 ml, 1 teaspoon = 5 ml.

Preheat ovens before use and cook on the centre
shelf unless cooking more than one item. If using
a fan oven, reduce the heat by 10–20°C, but check
with your handbook.

Medium eggs have been used.

This book contains recipes made with nuts.
Those with known allergic reactions to nuts and
nut derivatives, pregnant and breast-feeding
women and very young children should
avoid these dishes.

Contents

Introduction

There is something very cheering and pleasurable about gazing along a shelf of preserves that you have created. The colours and textures, as well as the tastes, are reminders of the raw ingredients, how you came about them and the seasons.

I have always dabbled in making preserves. I enjoy trying new recipes but relish the opportunity of repeating those that have been handed down over generations or of bringing a basic recipe bang up to date with a new twist.

Raspberry

Types of preserves

'Preserves' is a general term used to describe fruits and vegetables that have been preserved with the use of heat and sugar and/or vinegar and then stored in sealed jars.

Jams

Jams are fruit and sugar cooked to form a gel. Jams should be clear and bright and well set but not too stiff; they should have a distinct fruity flavour. A conserve is similar to jam except that the set is much softer and some fruits remain whole. Jellies use only the fruit juice. Because only the juice is used, the yield of a jelly is much lower than that of jam, making it rather more expensive. It is usually made and potted in small amounts and should be clear and sparkling.

Marmalade

Marmalade is a jam-like preserve, usually made with citrus fruits. Marmalade includes peel, which means it takes longer to cook. It also uses more water.

Curd

A curd is not a true preserve and not intended for keeping. Curds contain eggs and butter in addition to fruit and sugar and the cooking temperature, compared to other preserves, is very low. Curds can be stored in the refrigerator for up to six weeks. Once opened, they should be eaten within two weeks.

Pickles

In clear pickles, such as pickled onions, salt or brine is used to extract water from the vegetables, leaving them really crisp. They are then packed in vinegar, which can be plain, spiced or sweet. Sweet pickles are fruit or vegetables stewed in sweetened, spiced vinegar. In mixed pickles, such as piccalilli, vegetables are brined and then cooked in thickened spiced vinegar. All pickles need to be covered with vinegar-proof lids.

Chutney

A traditional cooked chutney can be based on almost any combination of fruit and vegetables, but it always contains acid, spices and a sweetener. In the UK, chutneys are usually cooked slowly to a jam-like consistency and then matured in the jar for a few weeks before use, to produce a mellow but fruity flavour full of character.

Relish

Relish contains similar ingredients to chutney but has a different texture and uses less vinegar. The vegetables for a relish are usually more coarsely chopped and are cooked for a shorter time or not cooked at all; therefore the texture has some of the crispness of the original. Relishes are not true preserves and they do not keep well for long. They can be eaten immediately after making and, once opened, should be kept in the fridge for no more than 2–3 weeks.

Making preserves

Pectin

Jams, jellies and marmalades depend on the right combination of pectin, acid and sugar to achieve a good set. Fruit will contain more or less acid and pectin according to the variety, freshness and degree of ripeness of the fruit, the season and the weather. Where low-pectin fruit is used, it is usually blended with a high-pectin fruit to achieve the right balance. High-pectin fruits include blackcurrants, redcurrants, cooking apples, gooseberries and some varieties of plum. Low-pectin fruits include strawberries, pears, cherries and late blackberries.

There is a very simple test to check the pectin content of the fruit pulp after simmering but before you add the sugar. Take a teaspoon of juice from the pan, pour it into a small glass lidded container and allow it to cool. Add a tablespoon of methylated spirit, add the lid and shake well. After about a minute, a transparent clot should form.

If the clot is large and jelly-like, the pectin content is high. No extra pectin is needed. If the clot is in two or three lumps, the pectin content is medium, but adequate for a set. If there is no clot, or if there are lots of very small ones, the pectin content is low. Extra pectin is needed. If a pectin test shows a low pectin level, add about 50–100 ml (2–3½ fl oz) of pectin stock for every 450 g (1 lb) of fruit. If using a commercial liquid pectin, follow the manufacturer's instructions.

Pectin stock

Don't throw away the peel, core and pips when preparing apples for your chutney or pies. Cover with water and cook gently for 45 minutes to an hour. Pour the contents of the pan through a jelly bag and allow to drip through – the resulting liquid is virtually tasteless pectin stock. Test it to make sure you have a good pectin level and then freeze in 300 ml (10 fl oz) containers. It is then ready to add to any jam needing pectin and will preserve the true taste of the fruit being used.

Setting

There are three simple ways of testing whether a jam, jelly or marmalade has reached setting point. It is important to keep the preserve off the heat during the test or it may go beyond the point of setting.

Stir the jam. Dip a sugar thermometer into hot water before dipping into the jam. If the temperature reaches 105°C/220°F, setting point should have been reached.

Chill a plate in the refrigerator. Put a teaspoon of jam on the plate and let it cool for 1 minute. Push the surface of the jam: if it wrinkles, the jam has reached setting point.

Dip a clean wooden spoon into the jam. Remove it and, holding it above the pan, twirl the spoon a few times to cool the jam. Let the jam fall off the spoon. If the drops run together and form flakes that 'hang' on the edge of the spoon, a setting point has been achieved.

Equipment

Most preserves need little specialist equipment, except perhaps a preserving pan. A heavy-based pan of good quality stainless steel will last a lifetime and it is worth paying as much as you can. The heavy base will help to prevent burning and the sloping sides and wider top help evaporation. The pan should only be about half full after the sugar has been added.

Most jars are reusable. If you are re-using old jars, check for any chips or cracks and then thoroughly wash the jars and remove any old labels. Wash the jars in hot, soapy water, rinse well in boiling water and turn upside-down to drain. Place on a cooling rack on a pad of kitchen towel and heat in the oven at 160°C/325°F/Gas Mark 3 for 10 minutes or until thoroughly dry. Leave to cool before filling. Alternatively, place the jars in a deep pan and cover with boiling water. Bring to the boil and boil for 10 minutes. Carefully remove and allow to drain and dry as above. It is also possible to sterilise jars in the microwave; follow the manufacturer's instructions for your model.

Coverings for preserves

The cheapest way to cover jams, jellies and marmalades is to use a waxed disc and cellophane cover secured with a rubber band. These are available in different sizes from most supermarkets, stationers and kitchen shops. Do not use twist tops with waxed discs and cellophane covers – the waxed disc will prevent the twist top from forming a correct seal.

Waxed discs and cellophane covers are not suitable for chutneys and other vinegar preserves, as they do not prevent evaporation. Use twist-top lids for these. They are widely available from kitchenware departments and shops. Scrupulously clean them before use: wash them in hot, soapy water and then rinse well. Then pour over boiling water and leave them in it for a few seconds before draining and drying thoroughly.

Twist-top lids must be applied as soon as the preserve is ready and potted. Fill the jar to the brim. As the preserve cools it shrinks and forms a vacuum. Waxed discs must also be applied immediately in order to melt the wax, which in turn forms a seal. Therefore it is essential that the disc fits the neck of the jar. The cellophane cover can be applied when the preserve is hot or cold and is simply a dust cover.

Label your preserves as soon as possible after the jars have cooled down and set. No matter how good your memory is – you will forget what's in unlabelled jars.

Tips for successful preserves

Jellies – Scald the jelly bag or cloth with boiling water first; then the juice will run through and not be absorbed by the fabric. You need to allow enough time for the jelly to drip through. Trying to hurry it along by squeezing the bag will often give a cloudy result.

Marmalade

Reduce the fruit mixture by at least half before adding the sugar. To achieve this, cover the fruit during the first stage of cooking, then cook uncovered to allow excess water to evaporate. To avoid having hard peel in the finished marmalade you must make sure that the fruit is very soft and squashy before adding the sugar. If you're using different varieties of citrus fruit then test each one – they do vary.

Sugar

It's a good idea to warm the sugar first, either in a low oven or in the microwave. Only add the sugar when the fruit is completely tender and the contents of the pan have reduced by about half. The golden rule for jam-making is slow cooking before the sugar is added and very rapid and short cooking afterwards.

Storage

Most preserves will keep for up to a year (and some for considerably longer) in a cool, dark and dry place. Once opened, the contents need to be eaten within 3–4 weeks and may be best kept in the fridge. Check opened jars regularly for any change in colour, signs of mould or deterioration or any unpleasant smell. If necessary, discard immediately.

Traditional strawberry jam

Strawberry jam is a sure winner and so evocative of our British summer. Serve with scones and clotted cream for a traditional tea time treat.

Makes 2.2 kg (5 lb)
Preparation and cooking time: about 45 minutes

1.3 kg (3 lb) **strawberries**, hulled and wiped, washed if necessary and drained really well
juice of 1 large **lemon** (about 2 tablespoons)
pectin
1.3 kg (3 lb) **granulated sugar**

Put the fruit in a large preserving pan with the lemon juice and simmer gently until the juices begin to run – about 10 minutes.

Mash the strawberries down with a potato masher and continue to simmer for another 5 minutes until the fruit is reduced to a thick purée.

Remove from the heat and carry out a pectin test (see page 8) and, if necessary, add pectin stock or a commercial pectin.

Add the sugar and stir until it is completely dissolved. Bring to the boil and boil for about 5 minutes before removing any scum and testing for a set (see page 8). If necessary, boil for longer and test again.

Pour into cooled, sterilised jars and then seal and label.

Tip Mashing the fruit helps to release the pectin, ensuring a good set. However, strawberry jam can be notoriously difficult to set, so you might need to add extra pectin.

Variations Strawberry and elderflower jam: Add 3–4 handfuls of elderflowers to the strawberries at the start.

Strawberry and lemongrass jam: Add 4 lemongrass stems, which have been lightly flattened with a rolling pin, to the strawberries as they cook. Remove the stems before potting the jam.

Strawberry jam with liqueur: Add 2 teaspoons of liqueur (such as Grand Marnier or Cointreau) to each jar before pouring in the hot jam.

Strawberry and gooseberry (or rhubarb) jam: Replace half of the strawberries with topped and tailed gooseberries or chopped rhubarb and add 150 ml (5 fl oz) of water. Cook the gooseberries or rhubarb in the water until they are quite tender – about 15 minutes. Add the strawberries and continue to simmer for about 5 minutes. Continue as in the main recipe.

Strawberry and redcurrant jam: Use 900 g (2 lb) of strawberries and 450 g (1 lb) of redcurrants, removed from their stems. Simmer the redcurrants in 575 ml (20 fl oz) of water until soft and then add the strawberries. Finish as in the main recipe.

Strawberry and passion fruit jam: Make the jam as in the main recipe and add the pulp of 4 passion fruits to the finished jam.

Traditional raspberry jam

This is so easy to make. It can be expensive if you have to buy the fruit, which is why I have included some variations with less expensive partners.

Makes about 2.2 kg (5 lb)
Preparation and cooking time: about 40 minutes

1.3 kg (3 lb) **raspberries**, washed and drained well if necessary
1.3 kg (3 lb) **granulated sugar**

Place the raspberries in a large preserving pan and simmer gently for about 10 minutes until the raspberries are tender and the juice is extracted.

Remove from the heat and add the sugar, stirring until it is completely dissolved.

Put the pan back on the heat and bring to the boil. Boil rapidly for about 5 minutes and then remove any scum. Test for a set (see page 8).

Pour into cooled, sterilised jars and then seal and label.

Variations
Raspberry and nectarine (or peach) jam: Replace half of the raspberries with 675 g (1½ lb) of chopped nectarines or peeled peaches and add 150 ml (5 fl oz) of water and 2 tablespoons of lemon juice. Cook the nectarines or peaches first with the water and lemon juice until soft – about 5 minutes. Add the raspberries and simmer for a further 5 minutes. Continue as in the main recipe.

Raspberry and rhubarb jam: Replace half the raspberries with rhubarb and add 150 ml (5 fl oz) of water. Cook for about 15 minutes before adding the raspberries. Continue as in the main recipe.

Orchard jam

This is a cross between jam and marmalade in texture and flavour. Layer with whipped cream and crushed meringue for a wonderful Eton mess.

Makes about 2.2 kg (5 lb)
Preparation time: 30 minutes
Cooking time: about 2½ hours

225 g (8 oz) **oranges**, juice squeezed, pips and peel reserved

225 g (8 oz) **grapefruits**, juice squeezed, pips and peel reserved

225 g (8 oz) **lemons**, juice squeezed, pips and peel reserved

350 g (12 oz) large **cooking apples**, peeled, cored and quartered, cores reserved

350 g (12 oz) large **pears**, peeled, cored and quartered, cores reserved

1.3 kg (3 lb) **granulated sugar**

Cut the citrus peel into thin strips. Tie the apple and pear cores and the citrus pips in a piece of muslin.

Put the fruit, juice, peel and muslin bag into a large preserving pan with 1.7 litres (3 pints) of water.

Bring to the boil and then simmer gently for 2 hours or until the fruit is very soft and the mixture is reduced by almost half.

Press the contents of the bag through a sieve and return the resulting thick purée to the pan. Add the sugar and stir until dissolved.

Bring to the boil and boil vigorously for about 15 minutes or until setting point is reached (see page 8). Remove any scum.

Pour into cooled, sterilised jars and then seal and label.

Tip The combined weight of all the fruits needs to be around 1.3 kg (3 lb), but don't worry if the proportion of each fruit varies slightly.

Hedgerow jam

The ingredients for this wonderful recipe can be found in hedgerows right across the countryside.

Makes about 2.2 kg (5 lb)
Preparation time: 30 minutes
Cooking time: about 1½ hours

225 g (8 oz) **rose hips**
225 g (8 oz) **haws**
225 g (8 oz) **rowan berries**
225 g (8 oz) **sloes**
450 g (1 lb) **crab apples**
450 g (1 lb) **blackberries**
450 g (1 lb) **elderberries**
115 g (4 oz) **hazelnuts**, chopped
900 g (2 lb) **granulated sugar**, plus equivalent to weight of fruit pulp

Wash all the fruit well. Put the rose hips, haws, rowan berries, sloes and crab apples in a large preserving pan and add water to cover. Bring to the boil and then simmer gently until all the fruit is tender – about 1 hour.

Sieve the fruits and weigh the resulting pulp. Put the pulp back into the washed preserving pan and add the blackberries, elderberries and chopped nuts. Simmer for about 15 minutes.

Add the sugar, plus as much extra sugar as the weight of the pulp. Cook over a low heat to dissolve the sugar and then boil rapidly for about 10 minutes or until setting point is reached (see page 8). Remove any scum.

Pour into cooled, sterilised jars and then seal and label.

Grape & apricot jam

This is delicious served with cold meats. Peaches can be used instead of apricots if you wish.

Makes about 1.3 kg (3 lb)
Preparation time: 20 minutes + 2–3 hours standing
Cooking time: about 40 minutes

225 g (8 oz) **black grapes**, halved and pips removed
225 g (8 oz) **green grapes**, halved and pips removed (or use 450 g/1 lb **seedless grapes**, halved, instead of both black and green grapes)
450 g (1 lb) **apricots**, halved and stoned
900 g (2 lb) **granulated sugar**
juice of 1 **lemon**
50 g (1¾ oz) **blanched almonds**, chopped (optional)
5 tablespoons **brandy**

Place the fruit and sugar in a large preserving pan. Leave to stand for 2–3 hours.

Slowly bring to the boil, stirring until the sugar is dissolved.

Add the lemon juice and then boil rapidly until setting point is reached (see page 8). Remove any scum. Add the almonds, if using, and the brandy.

Pour into cooled, sterilised jars and then seal and label.

Tip Apricot and almond is a favourite combination, but other nuts can be added to jam: how about walnuts with plum jam? Or stir toasted pine nut kernels into raspberry jam.

Plum & mulled wine jam

Mulled wine spices add a delicious flavour to this jam. Try it with warm, buttered, fruity toasted teacakes on an autumn day.

Makes 2.7 kg (6 lb)
Preparation time:
20 minutes
Cooking time:
about 30 minutes

1.8 kg (4 lb) **red plums**, halved and stoned
375 ml (13 fl oz) **red wine**
mulled wine spices (e.g. cinnamon, nutmeg, cloves or your own choice)
piece of **orange zest** without pith
1.8 kg (4 lb) **granulated sugar**

Put the plums and wine in a large preserving pan.

Place the spices and zest in a spice ball or muslin bag and add to the pan. Bring to the boil and then simmer gently for 15–20 minutes or until the plum skins are soft.

Remove the spice ball or bag and add the sugar, stirring until dissolved. Bring to the boil and boil rapidly for about 10 minutes or until setting point is reached (see page 8). Remove any scum.

Pour into cooled, sterilised jars and then seal and label.

Exotic fruits jam

A real taste of summer sunshine to brighten winter days! This lovely combination needs no pre-cooking before adding the sugar.

Makes 1.3–1.8 kg (3–4 lb)
Preparation time: 20 minutes
Cooking time: about 50 minutes

900 g (2 lb) ripe **pineapples**, skin and core removed, cut into 1 cm (½ inch) pieces

450 g (1 lb) **mangoes**, peeled, stoned and flesh cut into 1 cm (½ inch) pieces

grated zest and juice of 1 **lemon**, pips and pith reserved and tied in a muslin bag

1.3 kg (3 lb) **granulated sugar**

Place the fruit and its juices, lemon zest and 4 tablespoons of lemon juice (any remaining juice won't be needed), the muslin bag and the sugar in a large preserving pan. Heat gently and stir until all the sugar is dissolved.

Bring to the boil and then reduce the heat and simmer gently for 30–40 minutes, or until setting point is reached (see page 8). Remove any scum.

Pot into cooled, sterilised jars and then seal and label.

Tangier jam

This is a useful standby for winter when the fruit is finished and the store is empty. Served with ice cream, it makes a great topping for pancakes too.

Makes about 2.2 kg (5 lb)
Preparation time:
15 minutes + overnight soaking
Cooking time:
about 30 minutes

225 g (8 oz) **dried apricots**, chopped
450 g (1 lb) **raisins**
450 g (1 lb) **dates**, chopped
450 g (1 lb) **bananas** (peeled weight), chopped
1.8 kg (4 lb) **light brown soft sugar**

Cover the apricots and raisins with water and leave to soak overnight.

Drain away the water and place all the fruit in a large preserving pan. Simmer for 15 minutes.

Add the sugar and stir until dissolved.

Bring to the boil and boil rapidly until setting point is reached (see page 8). Remove any scum.

Pour into cooled, sterilised jars and then seal and label.

Orange & beetroot jam

This is a delicious combination that is a rather nice change from the usual. Serve on toast with grilled goat's cheese as an pretty snack or starter.

Makes 1.1–1.3 kg (2½–3 lb)
Preparation time: 20 minutes (if using ready cooked beetroot)
Cooking time: about 1 hour

900 g (2 lb) ready cooked **beetroot**, skinned and cut into strips
2 teaspoons grated **orange zest**
150 ml (¼ pint) **orange juice**
150 ml (¼ pint) **lemon juice**
½ teaspoon **ground cinnamon**
3 **oranges**, peeled and cut into segments, reserve peel, pith and any pips
900 g (2 lb) **granulated sugar**

Place the beetroot, orange zest, orange and lemon juices and cinnamon in a large preserving pan with 300 ml (10 fl oz) of water. Place the reserved peel, pith and pips in a muslin bag and add to the pan.

Bring to the boil and then simmer gently for 30 minutes.

Remove the bag and squeeze to extract all the juice. Add the sugar and stir until completely dissolved. Add the orange segments.

Boil rapidly for about 10 minutes or until setting point is reached (see page 8). Remove any scum. Leave to stand for 5–10 minutes.

Pour into cooled, sterilised jars and then seal and label.

Blackcurrant rhubarb jam

For this delicious combination of fruits, use rhubarb from the garden and blackcurrants from the freezer from the previous year.

Makes about 2.2 kg (5 lb)
Preparation and cooking time: about 1 hour

900 g (2 lb) **blackcurrants**, stalks removed
675 g (1½ lb) **rhubarb**, cut into 2.5 cm (1 inch) pieces
1.5 kg (3 lb 5 oz) **granulated sugar**

Place the fruit and 425 ml (15 fl oz) of water in a large preserving pan. Bring to the boil and then simmer gently until the fruit is quite soft – about 20 minutes. Remove from the heat.

Add the sugar and stir until dissolved.

Return to the heat and bring to the boil. Boil rapidly for 5–10 minutes or until setting point is reached (see page 8). Remove any scum.

Pour into cooled, sterilised jars and then seal and label.

Tutti frutti jam

The success of this jam is the combination of the pectin content of the different fruit. Make sure you cook the currants until they are really soft.

Makes about 2.7 kg (6 lb)
Preparation time: 30 minutes
Cooking time: 40 minutes

450 g (1 lb) **blackcurrants**, stalks removed
450 g (1 lb) **redcurrants**, stalks removed
450 g (1 lb) **strawberries**, hulled
450 g (1 lb) **raspberries**, hulled
1.8 kg (4 lb) **granulated sugar**

Place the blackcurrants and redcurrants in a large preserving pan with 150 ml (5 fl oz) of water. Bring to the boil and then gently simmer for 15–20 minutes, ensuring that the skins of the currants are soft.

Add the strawberries and raspberries and simmer for a further 10 minutes.

Add the sugar, stirring until dissolved. Bring to the boil and boil rapidly until setting point is reached (see page 8). Remove any scum.

Pour into cooled, sterilised jars and then seal and label.

Tip The best way to strip the currants from the stem is to hold the stalk in one hand and use a fork to slide down the stem and strip away the fruit.

Variations Midsummer jam: Replace the blackcurrants with gooseberries.

Four-fruit jam: Replace the redcurrants with gooseberries.

Rhubarb & fig jam

This unusual combination is a great way to use up any extra rhubarb growing in the garden.

Makes about 2.2 kg (5 lb)
Preparation and cooking time: about 55 minutes + overnight standing

1.3 kg (3 lb) **rhubarb**, cut into 2.5 cm (1 inch) pieces
1.3 kg (3 lb) **granulated sugar**
225 g (8 oz) dried **figs**, chopped
juice of 3 **lemons**

Place the rhubarb in a large non-metallic bowl and cover with the sugar. Leave overnight.

The next day, place the rhubarb, sugar, figs and lemon juice in a large preserving pan. Heat gently until the sugar has dissolved.

Bring to the boil and boil for about 30 minutes or until setting point is reached (see page 8). Remove any scum.

Ladle into cooled, sterilised jars and then seal and label.

Variation Rhubarb, orange and candied peel jam: Add finely chopped candied peel to the rhubarb and sugar before leaving overnight. Allow 40 g (1½ oz) of peel per 450 g (1 lb) of rhubarb.

Rhubarb & orange jam

This is one of the easiest and most delicious jams you can make. It looks great too, and would make an ideal addition to a Christmas hamper.

Makes about 2.2 kg (5 lb)
Preparation time: 40 minutes + 24 hours standing
Cooking time: about 1¾ hours

1.3 kg (3 lb) **rhubarb**, cut into 2.5 cm (1 inch) lengths
1.3 kg (3 lb) **granulated sugar**
grated zest and juice of 1 **lemon**
2 thin-skinned **oranges**

Put alternate layers of rhubarb and sugar into a non-metallic bowl. Add the lemon zest and juice. Cover and leave for 24 hours.

The next day, boil the whole oranges in 575 ml (20 fl oz) of water for about 1 hour or until they become translucent.

Cut five thin slices from the oranges and then chop the remaining fruit, discarding any pips.

Place the rhubarb and sugar mixture into a large preserving pan with the chopped oranges and bring slowly to the boil, stirring until the sugar has dissolved.

Boil rapidly until setting point is reached (see page 8), stirring only occasionally. Cool slightly and remove any scum. Stir again.

Fill each sterilised jar a quarter full and then slide an orange slice down the side of each jar. Fill to the brim carefully, without disturbing the orange slice. Seal and label on the side opposite the orange slice.

Variation Rhubarb, orange and ginger jam: Add 50–80 g (1¾–3 oz) of finely chopped stem ginger preserved in syrup or crystallised ginger.

High Dumpsy Dearie jam

I can't resist this recipe, even if just to preserve its name! No one knows where it comes from, but it makes a great base for steamed puddings.

Makes 3.2–3.6 kg (7–8 lb)
Preparation time: 30 minutes
Cooking time: about 1 hour

900 g (2 lb) **cooking apples**, peeled, cored and sliced
900 g (2 lb) **pears**, peeled, cored and sliced
900 g (2 lb) **plums**, halved and stoned
50 g (1¾ oz) **fresh root ginger**, bruised and tied in a muslin bag
2 kg (4½ lb) **granulated sugar**
grated zest and juice of 1 **lemon**

Place all the fruit and ginger in a large preserving pan and add just enough water to cover the base of the pan. Simmer until the fruit is tender – about 45 minutes.

Remove from the heat and add the sugar, stirring until dissolved. Add the lemon zest and juice.

Bring to the boil and boil rapidly for about 15 minutes or until setting point is reached (see page 8). Remove any scum.

Pour into cooled, sterilised jars, discarding the ginger, and then seal and label.

Mixed berry jam

This recipe needs no added sugar. Instead, it uses apple juice in concentrated form, which you can buy from health food shops.

**Makes about 675 g
  (1½ lb)**
**Preparation time:
  20 minutes**
**Cooking time:
  about 40 minutes**

225 g (8 oz) **strawberries**,
  fresh or frozen, hulled
225 g (8 oz) **blackberries**,
  fresh or frozen
225 g (8 oz) **gooseberries**
225 g (8 oz) **apple juice
  concentrate**

Liquidise half the fruit and place in a large preserving pan with the remaining whole fruit.

Simmer gently until the gooseberries are cooked – about 15–20 minutes.

Add the apple juice concentrate and boil for about 15 minutes or until setting point is reached (see page 8). Remove any scum.

Pour into cooled, sterilised jars and then seal. Label and store for up to 6 months. Once open, store in the fridge and use within 2 weeks.

Plum & grape jelly

A delicious jelly that goes very well with roast beef, as well as in the usual way as a spread.

Makes about 675 g (1½ lb)
Preparation time: 10 minutes + minimum 2 hours standing
Cooking time: about 1 hour

1.8 kg (4 lb) **plums**, any variety, stoned and chopped roughly
225 g (8 oz) **white grapes**
225 g (8 oz) **purple grapes**
1 tablespoon crushed **cardamom pods**
pectin (optional)
granulated sugar

Place the fruit and cardamom pods in a large preserving pan with 575 ml (20 fl oz) of water and bring slowly to the boil. Simmer until all the ingredients are cooked, mashing down the fruit occasionally to release all the flavours – about 30–45 minutes.

Pour into a jelly bag and leave to strain for a minimum of 2 hours. Measure the juice and do a pectin test (see page 8), adding pectin if necessary. To each 575 ml (20 fl oz) of juice, add 450 g (1 lb) of sugar.

Dissolve the sugar in the juice over a low heat. Bring to the boil and boil rapidly until setting point is reached (see page 8). Remove any scum.

Pour into cooled, sterilised jars and then seal and label.

Spiced apple jelly

A delicious recipe that goes well with roast pork or lamb as well as in tasty chunky sandwiches.

Makes about 900 g (2 lb)
Preparation time: 15 minutes + minimum 2 hours standing
Cooking time: about 1½ hours

900 g (2 lb) **cooking apples**, chopped, no need to peel or core
2 **lemons**, sliced
25 g (1 oz) **fresh root ginger**, chopped
1 **cinnamon stick**
½ teaspoon **cloves**
granulated sugar

Place the apples, lemons, ginger, cinnamon and cloves and 1.7 litres (3 pints) of water in a large preserving pan. Bring to the boil and simmer for 45–60 minutes, or until the apples are very soft.

Pour into a jelly bag and leave to strain for at least 2 hours. Measure the juice and add 450 g (1 lb) of sugar for each 575 ml (20 fl oz) of juice.

Dissolve the sugar in the juice over a gentle heat. Bring to a boil and boil rapidly until setting point is reached (see page 8). Remove any scum.

Pour into cooled, sterilised jars and then seal and label.

Blackberry & sloe jelly

A perfect autumn preserve and a different use for sloes. Try combing local hedgerows for blackberries rather than buying them from the shops.

Makes 1.3 kg (3 lb)
Preparation time:
20 minutes +
minimum 2 hours
standing
Cooking time: about
1 hour

1.8 kg (4 lb) **blackberries**
450 g (1 lb) **sloes**, washed
    and pricked with a needle
granulated sugar

Put the blackberries and sloes in a large preserving pan and cover with water. Bring to the boil and then reduce the heat and simmer gently until the sloes are tender – about 20 minutes but this may vary according to which end of the season the sloes were picked.

Pour into a jelly bag and leave to strain for at least 2 hours but preferably overnight. Measure the juice and add 450 g (1 lb) of sugar for each 575 ml (20 fl oz) of juice.

Dissolve the sugar in the juice over a gentle heat. Bring to a boil and boil rapidly until setting point is reached (see page 8). Remove any scum.

Pour into cooled, sterilised jars and then seal and label.

Gooseberry & mint jelly

This is a very useful alternative to apple jelly, as mint can be a bit sparse by the apple season. It works best with under-ripe or just-ripe gooseberries.

Makes about 1.1 kg (2¼ lb)
Preparation and cooking time: 1–1½ hours + overnight straining

1.3 kg (3 lb) **gooseberries**, no need to top and tail
a bunch of fresh **mint**, plus 2 tablespoons finely chopped fresh **mint**
425 ml (15 fl oz) **vinegar**
granulated sugar

Put the gooseberries in a large preserving pan with enough water to cover them. Add the bunch of mint and then bring to the boil and simmer until the gooseberries are soft – about 30 minutes.

Add the vinegar and cook for a further 5 minutes.

Pour into a jelly bag and leave to strain overnight. Measure the juice and add 450 g (1 lb) of sugar for each 575 ml (20 fl oz) of juice.

Dissolve the sugar in the juice over a gentle heat. Bring to a boil and boil rapidly for about 15 minutes or until setting point is reached (see page 8). Remove any scum.

Turn off the heat and cool slightly before stirring in the chopped mint.

Pour into small cooled, sterilised jars and then seal and label.

Tip Herb jellies are given extra appeal if you include either some of the chopped herb in the jelly or suspend a sprig in it. However, there can sometimes be a problem with the chopped herb or sprig rising in the jar. This recipe solves this by using the prepared herb wet, but not soaking, and adding it after setting point is reached.

Lemon curd

Use to fill a meringue pavlova or roulade, with whipped cream or half and half cream and Greek-style yogurt.

Makes about 1.3 kg (3 lb)
Preparation time: 15 minutes
Cooking time: about 10 minutes

200 g (7 oz) **butter**, preferably unsalted
700 g (1 lb 9 oz) **granulated** or **caster sugar**
grated zest of 4–5 **lemons**
300 ml (10 fl oz) **lemon juice** (about 4–5 lemons)
300 ml (10 fl oz) beaten **eggs** (about 4–5 eggs)

Place the butter, sugar, lemon zest and lemon juice in a large bowl and microwave on full power for about 2 minutes or until the butter has melted and the sugar has dissolved.

Add the beaten eggs and continue cooking in 1 minute bursts, stirring each time. Reduce to 30 seconds for each burst as the mixture thickens, until the mixture is thick enough to coat the back of the spoon.

Strain through a sieve into a wide-necked jug, to remove the lemon zest and any cooked egg bits. Put into cooled, sterilised jars, seal with a waxed disc and cover with cellophane. Label and store in the refrigerator.

Variations Passion fruit curd: Add the seeds and pulp of 4 ripe passion fruit just before potting.

Elderflower curd: Carefully strip the flowers from the stems of 2–3 handfuls of elderflowers and add to the curd when cooking.

West Country curd

Yet another way of capturing the last of the sunshine and a delicious alternative to the more traditional lemon curd.

Makes about 675–900 g (1½–2 lb)
Preparation time: 30 minutes
Cooking time: about 30 minutes

350 g (12 oz) **cooking apples**, cored and sliced, no need to peel

350 g (12 oz) **pears**, cored and sliced, no need to peel

grated zest and juice of 1 **lemon**

150 ml (5 fl oz) **cider**

350 g (12 oz) **granulated sugar**

115 g (4 oz) **butter**, preferably unsalted

4 **eggs**, beaten

Place the fruit and cider in a large bowl and cover with pierced cling film. Microwave on full power for 10–15 minutes or until the fruit is soft and pulpy.

Rub the fruit through a sieve and return to the bowl. Add the sugar and butter. Microwave on full power for 2 minutes and then stir well, making sure that the butter is melted and the sugar is dissolved.

Add the eggs and stir thoroughly. Continue cooking in the microwave until thick and the mixture coats the back of a spoon. Stir frequently. This can be done on full power or reduce the cooking power to medium and cook for a longer time.

Strain again into a jug to remove any bits of cooked egg. Pour the curd into cooled, sterilised jars, seal with a waxed disc and cover with cellophane. Label and store in the fridge for up to 6 weeks. Once opened, eat within 2 weeks.

Tip This can also be cooked in a double saucepan or in a bowl over a pan of simmering water – I just prefer to use the microwave.

Bramble & apple curd

This is quick and easy to make, a gorgeous colour and delicious to eat. Use it in the same way as lemon curd.

Makes about 1.1–1.3 kg (2–3 lb)
Preparation time: 20 minutes
Cooking time: about 20 minutes in the microwave or 40 minutes in a bowl over water

450 g (1 lb) **brambles** (blackberries)
450 g (1 lb) peeled, cored and chopped **cooking apples** (prepared weight)
grated zest and juice of 2 **lemons**
450 g (1 lb) **caster sugar**
4 **eggs**, beaten
115 g (4 oz) **butter**, preferably unsalted

Cook the fruit with the lemon zest and 2 tablespoons of water in a pan (or in the microwave) until pulpy. Purée the fruit by passing it through a sieve.

Transfer to a bowl if necessary, add the lemon juice and sugar and stir until the sugar is dissolved. Strain the eggs on to the fruit pulp.

Cook over a saucepan of water on a low heat or in the microwave, stirring occasionally, until a thick and creamy consistency is obtained. Strain the curd again to remove any bits of cooked egg.

Pour into cooled, sterilised jars, seal with a waxed disc and cover with cellophane. Label and store in the fridge for up to 6 weeks.

Tip I like to cook fruit curds in the microwave and prefer them to have a smooth consistency. Therefore, I usually sieve the fruit pulp to remove the bramble seeds and sieve again at the end, if necessary, to remove any cooked egg bits. If you prefer a chunkier result, simply mash the fruit down with a fork or potato masher.

Cranberry curd

This makes a curd with a fabulous colour and looks great on the Christmas breakfast table in a pretty pot or as a Christmas present.

Makes about 900 g (2 lb)
Preparation time: 10 minutes
Cooking time: about 30 minutes

450 g (1 lb) **cranberries**
115 g (4 oz) **unsalted butter**
450 g (1 lb) **caster sugar**
4 large **eggs**, beaten and sieved

Put the cranberries and 150 ml (5 fl oz) of water in a saucepan and cook on a low heat until tender and popped. (You could also cook them in the microwave).

Process them in a blender, or pass through a sieve if you prefer a smoother curd. Put back in the saucepan with the butter and sugar and heat until the butter is melted and the sugar is dissolved.

Add the eggs and stir the curd continuously over a low heat until thickened. If you are nervous of this, use a bowl over a pan of simmering water or the microwave (see Lemon Curd, page 44).

Pour into small, cooled, sterilised jars, seal with a waxed disc and cover with cellophane. Label and store in the fridge for up to 6 weeks. Once opened, eat within 2 weeks.

Gooseberry curd

Gooseberries make a lovely tangy curd. Some people prefer to keep in the skins and seeds of the fruit, but I prefer to sieve for a smooth curd.

Makes about 1.4 kg (3 lb)
Preparation time: 20 minutes
Cooking time: about 30 minutes

900 g (2 lb) **gooseberries**
450 g (1 lb) **granulated sugar**
115 g (4 oz) **butter**,
   preferably unsalted
4 eggs, beaten

Place the gooseberries and 2–3 tablespoons of water in a large bowl and cover with pierced cling film. Microwave on full power for 10–15 minutes or until very soft. Rub through a sieve to remove the skins and seeds.

Return to the bowl and add the sugar and butter. Cook on full power for 2 minutes or until the butter is melted and the sugar is dissolved.

Add the eggs and stir well. Cook in 1 minute bursts, stirring each time. Reduce to 30 seconds for each burst as the mixture thickens, until the mixture is thick enough to coat the back of the spoon.

Strain again, to remove any bits of cooked egg. Pour into cooled, sterilised jars, seal with a waxed disc and cover with cellophane. Label and store in the fridge for up to 6 weeks. Once opened, use within 2 weeks.

Seville orange marmalade

This is the traditional way of making marmalade. January into February is the time to make it, as this is the short season for fresh Seville oranges.

Makes about 4.5 kg (10 lb)
Preparation time: 1–1½ hours
Cooking time: about 2½ hours

1.3 kg (3 lb) **Seville oranges**
2 **lemons**
2.7 kg (6 lb) **granulated sugar**

Cut the fruit in half and squeeze out the juice. Remove the pips and membrane and tie them in a muslin bag.

Cut the peel into thin shreds (or coarse ones if preferred) and then place in a large preserving pan with the juice, bag of pips and 2.8 litres (5 pints) of water.

Bring to the boil and then simmer gently for about 2 hours, until the contents of the pan are reduced by about a half and the peel is really soft and tender.

Remove the muslin bag and squeeze hard and carefully so that all the gooey liquid enters the pan – this contains the pectin that is so important for a good set.

Add the sugar and stir until completely dissolved. Bring to the boil and boil rapidly until setting point is reached (see page 8).

Remove any scum. Cool for 5–10 minutes.

Stir well to distribute the peel. Pour into cooled, sterilised jars and then seal and label.

Variations Coriander marmalade: Add 1 tablespoon of crushed coriander seeds to the peel or pop them into the muslin bag.

Black treacle marmalade: Add 2 tablespoons or more of black treacle with the sugar.

Boozy marmalade: Stir in 2–4 tablespoons of whisky or other spirit or liqueur per 2.7 kg (6 lb) quantity just before potting. To achieve a variety of boozy flavours from one batch, put 10 ml (2 teaspoons) of a different spirit or liqueur into each jar before pouring in the hot marmalade.

Nutty marmalade: Add a few lightly toasted flaked almonds or chopped walnuts. Stir them in just before potting.

Extra-fruity marmalade: For an extra fruity flavour, add a couple of peeled, cored and chopped cooking apples about 10 minutes before the end of the simmering time, when cooking the fruit peel.

Ginger marmalade: Add 115 g (4 oz) of finely chopped, crystallised ginger, or stem ginger preserved in syrup, at the same time as the granulated sugar.

Pressure cooker marmalade

Cooking marmalade in a pressure cooker shortens the process of softening the peel. The same method can be used for other citrus-fruit marmalades.

Makes about 2.7 kg (6 lb)
Preparation time: 20 minutes
Cooking time: about 30 minutes

900 g (2 lb) **oranges**
2 **lemons**
1.8 kg (4 lb) **granulated sugar**

Cut the fruit in half and squeeze out and reserve all the juice, then cut the fruit into quarters and scrape out the remaining pulp and membrane. Put this, together with the fruit pips, in a muslin bag and tie loosely.

Place the fruit, juices, bag of pips and 575 ml (20 fl oz) of water in a pressure cooker. Bring to a medium (10 lb) pressure and cook for 10 minutes.

Reduce the pressure quickly and cool sufficiently to handle the fruit.

Discard the lemon peel and shred, slice or process the orange peel.

Squeeze the muslin bag really well to extract all the juice. Put the juice back into the cooker with another 575 ml (20 fl oz) of water and the prepared peel.

Bring to the boil in the open pressure cooker on a high heat. Add the sugar and stir until completely dissolved. Boil rapidly until setting point is reached (see page 8).

Pour into cooled, sterilised jars and then seal and label.

Caribbean marmalade

This combines wonderful citrus fruit and the black rum of the Caribbean for a popular marmalade.

Makes about 4.5 kg (10 lb)
Preparation time: 30 minutes
Cooking time: about 50 minutes

1.5 kg (3 lb 5 oz) mixture of **grapefruit, oranges, lemons** and 2 **limes**
3 kg (6½ lb) **granulated sugar**
black rum (it needs to be black and rough for the flavour)

Slice all the fruit and remove the pips. Place the fruit in a large pan with 2 litres (3½ pints) of water and simmer for 30–40 minutes until the peel is very soft. Take particular care that the lime peel is very tender, as it can become chewy when sugar is added.

Transfer the fruit and liquid to a large preserving pan and add the sugar, stirring until dissolved. Bring to a full rolling boil and test for a set (see page 8) after 5 minutes. It does set quite quickly – usually within 10 minutes. Remove any scum.

Put 2 teaspoons of rum per 450 g (1 lb) in the bottom of each of your cooled, sterilised jars and then pour in the marmalade. When the marmalade is poured in to fill the jar, the rum mixes in and gives a better flavour than if it was added to the jam pan.

Seal and label.

Tip This can be cooked in a large casserole in the oven. It is also very successful done in a slow cooker overnight, but reduce the amount of water used, remembering to add the remainder when you transfer to a preserving pan.

Citrus fruit marmalade

This can be made at any time of the year and is truly delicious. It uses whole lemons and just the flesh of the limes for a lovely flavour.

Makes about 4.5 kg (10 lb)
Preparation time: 20 minutes
Cooking time: about 40 minutes

675 g (1½ lb) mixed **orange, grapefruit** and **lemon peel**
450 g (1 lb) **whole lemons**
225 g (8 oz) **lime flesh**, pips and peel reserved
2.7 kg (6 lb) **granulated sugar**

Place the mixed peel and 300 ml (10 fl oz) of water in a pressure cooker and cook for 10 minutes at 15 lb pressure. Leave to cool to room temperature.

Drain, retaining the liquid, and slice the peel thinly when cool enough to handle. Set aside.

Cut the lemons into quarters, remove the pips and place these in a muslin bag. Remove and roughly chop the flesh and slice the peel thinly. Place in the pressure cooker.

Add the lime pips and peel to the lemon pips in the muslin bag. Chop the lime flesh roughly and add to the pressure cooker with the sealed muslin bag.

Add another 300 ml (10 fl oz) of water and cook for 10 minutes at 15 lb pressure. Allow to cool to room temperature.

Place the previously cooked peel and the lemon and lime flesh together in a large preserving pan. Squeeze the muslin bag thoroughly to extract all the juice. Mix together all the retained juices and add sufficient water to make up to 1.4 litres (2½ pints). Add to the preserving pan, along with the sugar.

Heat until the sugar is dissolved. Bring to the boil and boil rapidly until setting point is reached (see page 8). Remove any scum.

Pour into cooled, sterilised jars and then seal and label.

Ruby red marmalade

The colour of the grapefruit gives a lovely blush to this finished marmalade, so try to find the ruby red variety rather than just pink ones.

Makes 2.2–2.7 kg (5–6 lb)
Preparation time: 30 minutes
Cooking time: 2½–3 hours

900 g (2 lb) **ruby red grapefruit**, quartered
1 **lemon**, quartered
1.8 kg (4 lb) **granulated sugar**

Remove the grapefruit and lemon flesh from the peel and chop. Remove the pips and tie them in a muslin bag. If the peel is really thick, remove most of the pith and put it in the bag as well.

Cut all the peel finely and place in a large preserving pan with the chopped flesh, bag of pips and 1.1 litres (2 pints) of water. Bring to the boil and simmer until the peel is soft – about 1–2 hours.

Remove the muslin bag and squeeze to extract all the juice. Add the sugar and stir until dissolved. Bring to the boil and boil rapidly for about 20–30 minutes until setting point is reached (see page 8). Remove any scum.

Pour into cooled, sterilised jars and then seal and label.

Variations Ginger and grapefruit marmalade: Add 2 teaspoons of ground ginger and 115 g (4 oz) of chopped crystallised ginger or stem ginger preserved in syrup at the initial cooking stage.

Tipsy grapefruit marmalade: Add 4 tablespoons of any spirit or liqueur (try whisky, brandy, rum, Campari or a liqueur) just before potting.

Autumn marmalade

The apples give this marmalade an unusual texture. Make sure that you cook the citrus fruit well before adding the sugar and apples.

Makes 4.5 kg (10 lb)
Preparation time:
1 hour
Cooking time:
2–2½ hours

450 g (1 lb) **lemons**, chopped roughly after removing pips, pips reserved
450 g (1 lb) **limes**, chopped roughly after removing pips, pips reserved
675 g (1½ lb) **cooking apples**, peeled, cored and chopped
2.7 kg (6 lb) **granulated sugar**

Cut the lemons and limes in half and remove the pips. Place them in a muslin bag. Chop the fruit roughly.

Place the lemons, limes and muslin bag in a large preserving pan with 1 litre (1¾ pints) of water. Bring to the boil and simmer for about 2 hours, until the fruit is soft and the contents of the preserving pan are reduced in volume by about half.

Squeeze the bag of pips to extract the juice and set aside. Liquidise the fruit, using some of the liquid, until it is completely smooth. Return the purée to the pan and stir into the remaining cooking liquid.

Meanwhile, cook the apples over a very low heat until soft – you could use the microwave for this. Add to the citrus mixture with the granulated sugar.

Stir until the sugar is dissolved and then bring to the boil. Boil rapidly until setting point is reached (see page 8). Remove any scum.

Pour into cooled, sterilised jars and then seal and label.

Orange lemon marmalade

This is another recipe that uses apple juice concentrate (available from health food shops) rather than added sugar.

Makes about 450 g (1 lb)
Preparation time: 15 minutes
Cooking time: about 40 minutes

peel of 1 **orange**, sliced finely
peel of 1 **lemon**, sliced finely
425 ml (15 fl oz) freshly squeezed **orange juice** (commercial heat-treated orange juice is not suitable)
300 ml (10 fl oz) **apple juice concentrate**

Place the orange and lemon peels in a saucepan with the orange juice and simmer gently until the rind is soft – about 30 minutes.

Add the apple juice concentrate and continue to boil for 10 minutes. Test for a set (see page 8). Remove any scum.

When setting point is reached, pour into cooled, sterilised jars and seal. Label and store in the refrigerator.

Tip A good way of cleaning the skins of oranges and lemons is to scrub well in a solution of 1 tablespoon of cider vinegar to 575 ml (1 pint) of water. Rinse well and use as required.

Apricot orange marmalade

This is easily my favourite marmalade and that of my guests, once they've been persuaded to try something other than plain Seville orange.

Makes about 2.7 kg (6 lb)
Preparation time: 30 minutes
Cooking time: about 2½ hours

450 g (1 lb) no-need-to-soak **dried apricots**, sliced, chopped or snipped

675 g (1½ lb) **Seville oranges**, halved, squeezed of juice and sliced thinly, pips reserved

2.2 kg (5 lb) **granulated sugar**

Put the prepared fruit and 2 litres (3½ pints) of water in a large pan. Tie the pips and any membrane in a muslin bag and add to the pan. Bring to the boil and simmer until the fruit is very soft and the contents are reduced by about half. This will take about 2 hours.

Remove the muslin bag and squeeze to extract all the juice. Add the sugar and stir until dissolved. Bring to a rolling boil and boil for about 15–20 minutes until setting point is reached (see page 8).

Pour into cooled, sterilised jars and then seal and label.

Tip If using ordinary dried apricots, add an extra 300 ml (10 fl oz) of water and leave to stand for at least 6 hours or overnight before using.

Grapefruit marmalade

This is a wonderful and colourful marmalade. Dried cranberries are readily available in most supermarkets.

Makes about 4.5 kg (10 lb)
Preparation time: 30 minutes
Cooking time: about 2 hours

1.5 kg (3 lb 5 oz) **pink grapefruit**, sliced and pips removed
150 g (5 oz) **dried cranberries**
juice of 1 **lemon** or 2 teaspoons **citric acid**
3 kg (6½ lb) **granulated sugar**

Place the sliced grapefruit, cranberries, lemon juice or citric acid and 2 litres (3½ pints) of water in a large saucepan and simmer, covered, until the peel is very tender.

Transfer the fruit and liquid to a large preserving pan and add the sugar, stirring until dissolved. Bring to a full rolling boil and test for a set after 5 minutes. It does set quite quickly – usually within 10 minutes (see page 8). Remove any scum.

Pour into cooled, sterilised jars and then seal and label.

Tip This can be made in a large casserole in the oven. It is also very successful when done in a slow cooker overnight, but reduce the amount of water used, remembering to add the remainder when you transfer to a preserving pan.

Peach marmalade

This preserve is perfect with whipped cream as a Victoria sponge filling. The ratio of sugar to fruit means it is unsuitable for long keeping.

Makes about 1.3 kg (3 lb)
Preparation time: 40 minutes
Cooking time: about 45 minutes

2 **oranges**, chopped (or sliced if you prefer larger pieces of peel)
800 g (1¾ lb) **granulated sugar**
1.3 kg (3 lb) **peaches**, skinned, stoned and chopped
juice of 1 **lemon**

In a large pan, cook the oranges with 200 g (7 oz) of the sugar and 115 ml (4 fl oz) of water until they are soft.

Add the peaches with the rest of the sugar and the lemon juice. Stir until the sugar is dissolved. Bring to the boil and boil for about 15 minutes or until setting point is reached (see page 8). Remove any scum.

Pour immediately into cooled, sterilised jars and seal. Label and store in a cool and dry place for up to 6 months. Once opened, store in the fridge and use within 3–4 weeks.

Rum & raisin marmalade

This is a delicious recipe for grown ups. Adding the rum to the jars rather than to the marmalade produces a better flavour.

Makes about 4.5 kg (10 lb)
Preparation time: about 1 hour
Cooking time: about 2 hours

675 g (1½ lb) **sweet oranges**, sliced thinly
675 g (1½ lb) **lemons**, sliced thinly
175 g (6 oz) **raisins**
2.7 kg (6 lb) **granulated sugar**
rum

Place the citrus fruits in a large preserving pan with the raisins and 1.7 litres (3 pints) of water and bring to the boil.

Simmer slowly for 2 hours or until the peel is very tender.

Add the sugar and boil until setting point is reached (see page 8). Remove any scum.

Put 2 teaspoons of rum per 450 g (1 lb) of marmalade into cooled, sterilised jars. Pour in the marmalade and then seal and label.

Pumpkin marmalade

Pumpkin makes a lovely marmalade, with a beautiful colour. It's a great way of using up pumpkin flesh after carving Hallowe'en lanterns too.

Makes about 2.5 kg (5½ lb)
Preparation time: 30 minutes
Cooking time: about 1½ hours

1.5 kg (3 lb 5 oz) **pumpkin**, peeled, all seeds and fibre removed, and then flesh sliced

675 g (1½ lb) **oranges**, halved and sliced thinly

675 g (1½ lb) **lemons**, halved and sliced thinly

80 g (3 oz) **fresh root ginger**, shredded finely

1.3 kg (3 lb) **granulated sugar**

Place the pumpkin in a large pan with the oranges, lemons, ginger and 1 litre (1¾ pints) of water. Bring to the boil and then simmer for 45–60 minutes until the citrus peel is very soft.

Add the sugar, stirring until it has dissolved. Return to the boil and then cook over a medium heat until the mixture is thick enough for a wooden spoon to be drawn through the centre to leave a clear channel.

Pour the marmalade into cooled, sterilised jars and then seal and label.

Tomato & celery chutney

This is a lovely chutney. Celery marries very well with the tomatoes, making it an ideal accompaniment to cheeses, especially a good strong one.

Makes about 2.7 kg (6 lb)
Preparation time: 45 minutes
Cooking time: 2–2½ hours

450 g (1 lb) **onions**, chopped finely
1 large or 2 small heads of **celery**, trimmed and chopped finely
900 ml (1½ pints) **malt vinegar**
50 g (1¾ oz) **whole pickling spices**, tied in muslin
1 kg (2¼ lb) **ripe tomatoes**, skinned and chopped
450 g (1 lb) **cooking apples**, peeled, cored and finely chopped or processed
2 teaspoons **salt**
a good pinch of **cayenne pepper**
350 g (12 oz) **light brown soft sugar**
225 g (8 oz) **sultanas** or **raisins**, chopped roughly

Place the onions, celery, half the vinegar and the bag of spices in a large preserving pan. Bring to the boil and then simmer for about 30 minutes until almost tender.

Add all the other ingredients with the remaining vinegar. Bring slowly to the boil, stirring frequently, and continue to cook slowly for 1½–2 hours, or until the chutney is thick and there is no liquid left on the surface. Stir from time to time to prevent sticking.

Remove the bag of spices and spoon the chutney into cooled, sterilised jars. Seal with vinegar-proof lids. Label and store for 2–3 weeks before use.

Apricot & marrow chutney

This is perfect if you are inundated with marrows. In the reverse situation – a glut of apples instead of marrows – just double the amount of apples.

Makes about 2.2 kg (5 lb)
Preparation time: 30 minutes + soaking
Cooking time: about 1½ hours

450 g (1 lb) **dried apricots**, chopped
450 g (1 lb) prepared **marrow**, diced
450 g (1 lb) **cooking apples**, peeled, cored and quartered
350 g (12 oz) **onions**, chopped
2 teaspoons each whole **cloves**, **cardamom pods** and **peppercorns**
80 g (3 oz) **fresh root ginger**, bruised
575 ml (20 fl oz) **white malt vinegar**
450 g (1 lb) **granulated sugar**

Cover the apricots with water and soak for several hours or overnight. If you have 'no-need-to-soak' apricots, you can omit this step.

Tip the apricots into a large preserving pan. Add the marrow, apples and onions. Tie the whole spices and ginger in a piece of muslin and add to the mixture. Cook until the apples are pulpy, adding more water if necessary to prevent sticking and stirring occasionally. This will take about 20 minutes.

Add the vinegar and sugar and simmer until all the liquid has been absorbed.

Pot into cooled, sterilised jars, seal with vinegar-proof lids and label. Store for 6–8 weeks before using.

Variation Apricot, marrow and walnut chutney: Add 115 g (4 oz) of chopped walnuts towards the end of the cooking time.

Mango chutney

Serve with any curry or tandoori dishes or cold cuts. It can be used immediately but will develop even more flavour on keeping.

Makes about 1.3 kg (3 lb)
Preparation time: 30 minutes
Cooking time: 20 minutes

1 tablespoon **raisins**
6 **dried chillies**, ground or crumbled
2.5 cm (1 inch) **fresh root ginger**, grated
1 teaspoon **chilli powder**
1 teaspoon **black peppercorns**, lightly crushed
115 ml (4 fl oz) **vinegar**
225 g (8 oz) **granulated sugar**
3 teaspoons **salt**
2 **garlic cloves**, crushed
6 **green mangoes**, peeled, stoned and sliced

Soak the raisins in just enough water to cover them for 10–15 minutes.

Mix together the chillies, ginger, chilli powder and peppercorns.

Boil together the vinegar, sugar and salt. Add the chilli mixture, garlic and 115 ml (4 fl oz) of water. Cook for 2 minutes.

Add the mangoes and simmer for 10–12 minutes. Add the drained raisins.

Spoon into cooled, sterilised jars, seal with vinegar-proof lids and label.

South seas chutney

Ripe mangoes are the best choice for this chutney as they break down more easily. Raspberry vinegar and lime juice add that indefinable something.

Makes about 1.5 kg (3 lb 5 oz)
Preparation time: 30 minutes
Cooking time: about 2 hours

450 g (1 lb) **onions**, chopped
300 ml (10 fl oz) **raspberry vinegar**
300 ml (10 fl oz) **white wine vinegar**
3 **mangoes**, peeled, stoned and chopped
432 g can **crushed pineapple in natural juice**
1 tablespoon grated **fresh root ginger**
3 teaspoons **ground ginger**
2 teaspoons **ground coriander**
1 teaspoon **ground cumin**
½ teaspoon **ground cloves**
½ teaspoon **ground allspice**
2 teaspoons **lime juice**
50 g (1¾ oz) **sultanas**
450 g (1 lb) **golden granulated sugar**
25 g (1 oz) **flaked almonds**

Gently cook the onions in both vinegars for 5 minutes. Add the mangoes, pineapple with juice, ginger, spices and lime juice and cook until soft – about 40 minutes to 1 hour.

Add the sultanas and cook for a further 15 minutes.

Add the sugar and cook until reduced and there is no free vinegar. Add the almonds.

Spoon into cooled, sterilised jars, seal with vinegar-proof lids and label. Store for 6–8 weeks before using.

Green tomato chutney

There must be so many green tomatoes come autumn because there seems to be a never-ending supply of recipes for green tomato chutney.

Makes about 2.7 kg (6 lb)
Preparation time: 30 minutes + overnight
Cooking time: about 2 hours

1.3 kg (3 lb) **green tomatoes**, finely chopped
675 g (1½ lb) **cooking apples**, peeled cored and finely chopped
675 g (1½ lb) **onions**, finely chopped
2 tablespoons **salt**
575 ml (20 fl oz) **malt vinegar**
350 g (12 oz) **granulated sugar**
2 teaspoons **ground mixed spice**
225 g (8 oz) **sultanas**

Put the tomatoes, apples and onions in a large bowl and sprinkle over the salt. Cover and leave overnight.

The next day, pour off the liquid that has been drawn out by the salt and discard it. Transfer everything to a large preserving pan. Add the vinegar, bring to the boil and then add the sugar, spice and sultanas.

Bring back to the boil and simmer until soft and pulpy, about 1½ hours.

Spoon into cooled, sterilised jars, seal with vinegar-proof lids and label. Store for 6–8 weeks before using.

Nectarine chutney

This is cooked in the oven and quite strongly flavoured with rosemary, so you could reduce this if you wish. It can be made with any fruit.

Makes about 1.3 kg (3 lb)
Preparation time: 30 minutes
Cooking time: about 1¾ hours

1.1 kg (2¼ lb) **nectarines**, about 12 fruits, stoned and quartered
675 g (1½ lb) **red onions**, sliced finely
4 **garlic cloves**, chopped roughly
1 **lemon**, halved and pips removed, sliced finely
2 tablespoons chopped **fresh rosemary**
1 teaspoon **cumin seeds**
1 teaspoon **fennel seeds**
250 ml (9 fl oz) **cider vinegar**
500 g (1 lb 2 oz) **demerara sugar**

Preheat the oven to 200°C/400°F/Gas Mark 6.

Put all the ingredients except the sugar into a large roasting tin. Mix well and roast for 1¼ hours, stirring occasionally.

When the mixture starts to reduce and colour, add the sugar. Cook for a further 30 minutes, stirring twice during this period. The chutney should be fairly dry and any liquid should be quite syrupy and jam-like. The shapes of the fruit should still be discernible.

Spoon into cooled, sterilised jars and seal with vinegar-proof lids. Label and store.

Tip This could be used straightaway but the flavour will mature on keeping.

Easter chutney

Originally called Eastern chutney, this is a good example of how names change as they are handed on.

Makes about 1.8 kg (4 lb)
Preparation and cooking time: about 1 hour

450 g (1 lb) **oranges** (about 3–4 oranges)
450 g (1 lb) **onions**, chopped
450 g (1 lb) **stoned dates**
225 g (8 oz) **sultanas**
675 g (1½ lb) **demerara sugar**
2 teaspoons **salt**
½ teaspoon **cayenne pepper**
575 ml (20 fl oz) **malt vinegar**

Remove the zest from 1 orange using a potato peeler and set aside.

Peel all the oranges, removing as much pith as possible. Chop the fruit roughly and discard the pips and the peel (or pop it in a bag in the freezer to make marmalade later).

Coarsely mince (or use a food processor to shred) the onions, dates, orange flesh and reserved orange zest and set aside.

Put the sultanas, sugar, salt, cayenne pepper and vinegar into a large preserving pan. Bring the mixture to the boil and add the minced or shredded mixture.

Return to the boil and then reduce the heat and simmer until the chutney is thick and free of liquid – about 30 minutes.

Spoon the chutney into cooled, sterilised jars and seal with vinegar-proof lids. Label and store for 6–8 weeks before use.

Pumpkin chutney

Pumpkin makes a beautiful chutney that goes perfectly with cold meats. The texture can be varied by cutting the fruits into larger pieces.

Makes about 2.7 kg (6 lb)
Preparation time: 30 minutes
Cooking time: 2–2½ hours

675 g (1½ lb) peeled and de-seeded **pumpkin**
450 g (1 lb) **cooking apples**
350 g (12 oz) **onions**, chopped
175 g (6 oz) **sultanas** or **raisins**
2 tablespoons **salt**
2 teaspoons **ground ginger** or 50 g (1¾ oz) fresh root ginger, shredded finely
½ teaspoon **ground black pepper**
2 teaspoons **ground allspice**
4–6 **garlic cloves**, crushed
575 ml (1 pint) **malt** or **cider vinegar**
450 g (1 lb) **granulated** or **light brown soft sugar**
50 g (2 oz) **stem ginger** preserved in syrup, chopped finely (optional)

Cut the pumpkin into 2.5 cm (1 inch) chunks and peel, core and chop the apples coarsely.

Put all the ingredients, except the sugar and stem ginger, in a large preserving pan and mix well.

Bring to the boil and then reduce the heat and simmer for about 45 minutes, stirring occasionally, until the mixture is very soft.

Stir in the sugar until dissolved and then continue to simmer for about 1–1½ hours or until the chutney is very thick and there is no liquid left on the surface.

Add the stem ginger, if using. Spoon into cooled, sterilised jars and seal with vinegar-proof lids. Label and store for 6–8 weeks before use.

Tip Some cooks prefer to tie whole spices into a muslin bag, which is removed before potting the chutney. Others prefer to use the ground spices, although this tends to give a cloudier result.

Variation If you want a hotter chutney, add 3–4 fresh red chillies, finely chopped, and 2–3 tablespoons of mustard seeds.

Spiced plum chutney

This is delicious served with smoked mackerel. The cooking time can be reduced by cooking the plums, apples and onions in the microwave first.

Makes about 1.8 kg (4 lb)
Preparation time: about 30 minutes
Cooking time: about 1 hour

675 g (1½ lb) **plums**, stoned and quartered
450 g (1 lb) **onions**, chopped
225 g (8 oz) **cooking apples**, peeled, cored and chopped
300 ml (10 fl oz) **pickling vinegar**
115 g (4 oz) **sultanas**
175 g (6 oz) **light brown soft sugar**
1 **cinnamon stick**

Place all the ingredients in a large preserving pan. Bring to the boil and simmer, uncovered, for about 45 minutes, or until the chutney is thick and pulpy.

Spoon into cooled, sterilised jars and seal with vinegar-proof lids. Label and store for at least 4–6 weeks before use.

Cranberry chutney

This makes a lovely and colourful accompaniment to traditional Christmas fare and would make a very acceptable gift.

Makes 1.3 kg (3 lb)
Preparation time:
  20 minutes
Cooking time:
  1½–2 hours

25 g (1 oz) **butter**
350 g (12 oz) **onions**, chopped
450 g (1 lb) **cooking apples**, peeled, cored and sliced
1 teaspoon **ground mixed spice**
350 g (12 oz) fresh or frozen **cranberries**
450 g (1 lb) **light brown soft sugar**
425 ml (15 fl oz) **white malt vinegar**

Melt the butter in a large saucepan. Add the onions, apples and spice and cook until the onions are soft – about 20 minutes.

Add the cranberries and sugar and stir until the sugar is dissolved. Add the vinegar and bring to the boil, stirring occasionally.

Reduce the heat and simmer for 1–1½ hours, until the chutney is reduced to a thick pulpy consistency.

Spoon into cooled, sterilised jars and seal with vinegar-proof lids. Label and store for 4–6 weeks before using.

Gooseberry chutney

Try cooking the gooseberries and onions in the microwave first to reduce the total cooking time. Use red gooseberries for a good colour.

Makes about 2 kg (4½ lb)
Preparation time: 1 hour
Cooking time: about 45 minutes

1.3 kg (3 lb) **gooseberries**
225 g (8 oz) **onions**, chopped roughly
225 g (8 oz) **sultanas**
20 g (¾ oz) **salt**, or less if preferred
450 g (1 lb) **sugar**
850 ml (1½ pints) **malt vinegar**
1 tablespoon **allspice berries**
1 tablespoon **ground ginger**
¼ teaspoon **cayenne pepper**

Place all the ingredients in a large preserving pan. Bring to the boil and then reduce the heat and simmer until the chutney is of a thick and pulpy consistency, about 45 minutes.

Spoon into cooled, sterilised jars and seal with vinegar-proof lids. Label and store for at least 4–6 weeks before using.

Variation Substitute tarragon vinegar for half the malt vinegar, for a different flavour.

Rhubarb & date chutney

This is a good recipe to make earlier in the year. It is particularly delicious in a strong flavoured cheese sandwich or with cold meats.

Makes about 3 x 450 g (1 lb) jars
Preparation time: about 20 minutes
Cooking time: 1–2 hours

900 g (2 lb) **rhubarb**, cut into 5 cm (2 inch) chunks
450 g (1 lb) **onions**, chopped roughly
115 g (4 oz) **dates**, chopped
300 ml (10 fl oz) malt vinegar
450 g (1 lb) **granulated** or **demerara sugar**
1 level tablespoon **salt**
1 level tablespoon **ground ginger**
½ teaspoon **cayenne pepper**

Place all the ingredients in a large saucepan with 300 ml (10 fl oz) of water and bring to the boil. Reduce the heat and simmer gently for 1–2 hours or until the chutney has a jam-like consistency and there is no excess liquid on the surface. Stir from time to time to prevent sticking.

Allow to cool slightly.

Spoon into cooled, sterilised jars and seal with vinegar-proof lids. Label and store for 6–8 weeks before use.

Variations Rhubarb and garlic chutney: Add 2 crushed cloves of garlic and the zest of 1 orange and 1 lemon.

Rhubarb and ginger chutney: Omit the dates and add 50 g (1¾ oz) of finely chopped stem ginger preserved in syrup or crystallised ginger.

Rhubarb and apricot, raisin or sultana chutney: Replace the dates with chopped dried apricots or with raisins or sultanas.

Orchard cottage chutney

This recipe certainly brings together traditional autumn fruits and vegetables and conjures up a country feel with its title.

Makes 2.7 kg (6 lb)
Preparation time: about 45 minutes
Cooking time: about 2 hours

900 g (2 lb) **plums**, washed, halved and stoned
900 g (2 lb) ripe **tomatoes**, skinned and sliced
850 ml (1½ pints) **malt vinegar**
6 **garlic cloves**
450 g (1 lb) **onions**, chopped roughly
225 g (8 oz) **raisins**
1.1 kg (2¼ lb) **cooking apples**, peeled and cored
450 g (1 lb) **demerara sugar**
25 g (1 oz) **salt**
50 g (2 oz) **whole pickling spices**, tied in a muslin bag

Put the plums, tomatoes and vinegar into a large preserving pan. Bring to the boil and then simmer gently until very soft.

Mince together the garlic, onions, raisins and apples, or use a food processor to chop them finely. Add to the plum mixture with the sugar, salt and bag of spices.

Heat gently until the sugar is dissolved. Bring to the boil and then simmer, uncovered, for about 2 hours, or until the chutney is well reduced and very thick. Stir from time to time to prevent sticking.

Spoon into cooled, sterilised jars and seal with vinegar-proof lids. Label and store for 2–3 weeks before use.

Ratatouille chutney

This is one of my favourite chutney recipes – a strong and hot chutney that uses a variety of produce from the garden.

Makes about 4 x 450 g (1 lb) jars
Preparation time: 45 minutes
Cooking time: 2–2½ hours

900 g (2 lb) **tomatoes**, skinned and chopped
450 g (1 lb) **Spanish onions**, chopped
450 g (1 lb) **courgettes**, sliced thinly
1 large **green pepper**, de-seeded and sliced
1 large **red pepper**, de-seeded and sliced
1 **aubergine**, diced
2 large **garlic cloves**, crushed
1 tablespoon **salt**
1 tablespoon **cayenne pepper**
1 tablespoon **paprika**
1 tablespoon **ground coriander**
300 ml (10 fl oz) **malt vinegar**
350 g (12 oz) **granulated sugar**

Place the tomatoes, onions, courgettes, peppers, aubergine and garlic in a large pan. Add the salt, cayenne pepper, paprika and coriander. Cover and cook gently, stirring occasionally, until the juices run.

Bring to the boil, reduce the heat, uncover and simmer for 1–1½ hours or until the vegetables are soft but still recognisable as shapes and most of the water from the tomatoes has evaporated.

Add the vinegar and sugar, stirring to dissolve the sugar. Continue to cook for 1 hour or until the chutney is thick and there is no free vinegar on top.

Spoon while still hot into cooled, sterilised jars and seal with vinegar-proof lids. Label and store for at least 2 months before using.

Beetroot & ginger chutney

This is one of the first chutneys I ever made and it remains one of my favourites. Serve with hot or cold meats such as roast pork.

Makes about 2.2–2.7 kg (5–6 lb)
Preparation time: about 40 minutes
Cooking time: about 2 hours

1.3 kg (3 lb) **beetroot**, cooked
450 g (1 lb) **onions**, chopped
1.1 litres (2 pints) **vinegar**
450 g (1 lb) **cooking apples**, peeled, cored and chopped
450 g (1 lb) **seedless raisins** or **dates**, chopped
3 tablespoons **ground ginger**
1 teaspoon **salt**
900 g (2 lb) **granulated sugar**

Peel and cut the beetroot into cubes or mash well if a smoother chutney is preferred.

Place the onions in a large preserving pan with a little of the vinegar and cook for a few minutes to soften. Add the apples, raisins or dates and continue cooking until pulpy.

Add the beetroot, ginger, salt and half the remaining vinegar. Simmer gently until thick.

Stir in the sugar and remaining vinegar and continue cooking until thick again.

Pot into cooled, sterilised jars, seal with vinegar-proof lids and label. Store for 6–8 weeks before using.

Storecupboard chutney

The ingredients for this recipe can vary, depending on the type of dried fruit you have in your cupboard at the time of making.

Makes about 2.2 kg (5 lb)
Preparation time: 30 minutes
Cooking time: about 1 hour

675 g (1½ lb) **mixed dried fruit** (e.g. apricots, dates, figs, peaches, prunes, sultanas), cut into even sized pieces
1.3 kg (3 lb) **cooking apples**, peeled, cored and chopped
450 g (1 lb) **onions**, chopped
675 g (1½ lb) **light brown soft sugar**
6 **garlic cloves**, crushed or chopped
50 g (1¾ oz) **fresh root ginger**, finely chopped
2–4 **dried chillies**, crushed
850 ml (1½ pints) **cider vinegar**

Mix everything together in a large preserving pan and bring to the boil, stirring well.

Simmer the mixture over a medium heat until very thick, stirring regularly – about 45 minutes.

Spoon into cooled, sterilised jars and seal with vinegar-proof lids. Label and store for 6–8 weeks before using.

Uncooked chutney

I have always steered away from uncooked chutneys and relishes, but those that I have tasted have always been very good.

Makes about 2.2 kg (5 lb)
Preparation time: 20 minutes + overnight soaking

225 g (8 oz) **dried apricots**
900 g (2 lb) **Bramley cooking apples**, peeled, cored and chopped
225 g (8 oz) **sultanas**
225 g (8 oz) **dates**, stoned
450 g (1 lb) **onions**, chopped
2 **garlic cloves**
350 g (12 oz) **light brown soft sugar**
425 ml (15 fl oz) **malt vinegar**
1 teaspoon **ground ginger**

Place the apricots in a bowl and cover with water. Leave to soak overnight and then drain. If you use 'no-need-to-soak' dried apricots, you can omit this step.

Mince all the fruits, onions and garlic together or finely chop in a food processor. Add the sugar, vinegar and ginger.

Stir well and spoon into cooled, sterilised jars. Seal with vinegar-proof lids and label. Store in a cool, dark place for at least 3 months before using.

Mango pickle

A change from the usual mango chutney and is an excellent way to preserve mangoes. It goes well with spicy dishes like Cajun chicken.

**Makes 6 x 450 g
  (1 lb) jars
Preparation time:
  45 minutes
Cooking time:
  about 20 minutes**

3.6 kg (8 lb) **ripe mangoes**, peeled
pared zest of ½ a **lemon**
15 g (½ oz) **whole cloves**
15 g (½ oz) **whole allspice berries**
7 g (¼ oz) **fresh root ginger**
7 g (¼ oz) **cinnamon stick**
1.1 litres (2 pints) **distilled** or **malt vinegar**
1.8 kg (4 lb) **granulated sugar**

Cut slices of flesh from the mangoes down to the stone, so that each mango provides 10–12 slices.

Place the lemon zest and spices in a muslin bag and secure.

Place the vinegar and sugar in a large preserving pan and heat slowly, stirring continuously, until all the sugar has dissolved.

Add the fruit and the bag of spices and simmer until the fruit is tender but not too soft.

Remove the bag of spices and drain the fruit. Pack into cooled, sterilised jars. Pour the syrup back into the pan and bring to the boil.

Boil the syrup until it starts to thicken and then pour over the fruit. Seal with vinegar-proof lids. Keep any leftover vinegar syrup and use to top up the jars if necessary, as the fruit absorbs the liquid on standing. Allow to mature for at least 1 month before using.

Gentleman's relish

This is great as a Christmas present. Spread on melba toast for a delicious snack or serve as a nibble at a drinks party.

Makes 225 g (8 oz)
Preparation time:
  15 minutes

3 x 50 g cans **anchovy fillets**
6 tablespoons **milk**
150 g (5½ oz) **unsalted**
  butter
freshly ground black
  pepper
cayenne pepper

Drain the anchovy fillets and soak in the milk for 10 minutes.

Drain off the milk and put the anchovies in a food processor or blender with the butter, black pepper and cayenne pepper.

Purée to a smooth paste. Pot into small, cooled, sterilised pots or jars, seal and store in the fridge for up to 3 weeks.

WOW mincemeat

WOW – walnut, orange and whisky. This has become a firm favourite. For a sharper taste, you could substitute cranberries for half the apple.

Makes about 1.3 kg (3 lb)
Preparation time: 30 minutes + overnight standing
Cooking time: about 15 minutes

450 g (1 lb) **cooking apples**, peeled, cored and chopped
225 g (8 oz) **sultanas**
225 g (8 oz) **currants**
115 g (4 oz) **candied peel**
115 g (4 oz) **walnut pieces**
175 g (6 oz) **melted butter** or **suet**
225 g (8 oz) **light muscovado sugar**
juice and grated zest of 1 large **orange**
1 teaspoon **ground cinnamon**
½ teaspoon **grated nutmeg**
½ teaspoon **ground cloves**
4 tablespoons **whisky**

Cook the apples with 4 tablespoons of water until pulpy. Mash down and allow to cool.

Add the rest of the ingredients and mix well. Allow to stand overnight.

Pack into cooled, sterilised jars and seal with waxed discs and cellophane covers, or store in the fridge in a polythene tub with a lid.

Christmas mincemeat

This is very quick to make. It contains no added sugar or fat but, of course, the dried fruit has a high sugar content and may also have a coating of oil.

Makes about 1.8 kg (4 lb)
Preparation time: 20 minutes
Cooking time: about 20 minutes

900 g (2 lb) **mixed dried fruit**
450 g (1 lb) **cooking apples**, peeled, cored and grated
2 teaspoons **ground mixed spice**
575 ml (20 fl oz) **medium sweet** or **dry cider**
50 g (1¾ oz) **hazelnuts**, chopped (optional)
2 tablespoons **brandy**

Simmer the dried fruits, apples and spice in the cider for about 20 minutes, or until the fruit is pulpy and most of the liquid has evaporated.

Stir in the hazelnuts and brandy.

Pack into cooled, sterilised jars and seal with a waxed disc and cellophane cover, or store in a polythene tub with a lid. Keep in a cool place or the refrigerator until required. It keeps for up to 4 months.

Cumberland bean pickle

This uses similar ingredients to piccalilli, but the vegetables are simply cooked in lightly salted water before being mixed with the sauce.

Makes about 6 x 450 g (1 lb) jars
Preparation and cooking time: about 1 hour

900 g (2 lb) trimmed and thinly sliced **runner beans** (prepared weight)
450 g (1 lb) **onions**, sliced finely
a pinch of **salt**
425 ml (15 fl oz) **white malt vinegar**
50 g (1¾ oz) **plain flour**
1 tablespoon **mustard powder**
½ teaspoon **ground black pepper**
½ teaspoon **turmeric**
150 g (5½ oz) **caster sugar**

Put the beans and onions in a pan with a pinch of salt and just enough water to cover. Bring to the boil and then simmer until tender – about 20 minutes.

In another large pan, mix together a tablespoon of vinegar, the flour and the spices to a smooth paste. Start to heat gently, adding the rest of the vinegar very carefully bit by bit, as you would for a roux sauce, ensuring that there are no lumps.

Simmer gently for 2–3 minutes, until the flour is cooked.

Add the sugar and stir well to make sure it is dissolved. Bring the sauce to the boil. It should be thick and shiny.

Drain the beans and onions and add to the sauce. Stir well and bring the mixture back to the boil. Continue cooking for about 10 minutes.

Spoon the mixture into cooled, sterilised jars and seal with vinegar-proof lids. Label and store.

Variations Carrot and runner bean pickle: Add 450 g (1 lb) of peeled and sliced carrots and cook along with the beans and onions.

Add more sugar if you prefer a sweeter pickle. This also works well with broad beans and French beans.

Piccalilli

This recipe works beautifully, produces a lovely piccalilli and keeps well if you can persuade the family to leave it for at least 2 weeks!

Makes about 2.7 kg (6 lb)
Preparation time: 30 minutes
Cooking time: about 30 minutes

1 large **cauliflower**, broken into florets
450 g (1 lb) **pickling onions**, chopped
1.4 litres (2½ pints) **white malt vinegar**
900 g (2 lb) **mixed vegetables**, diced or cut into 2.5 cm (1 inch) lengths (choose from French or runner beans, cucumber, marrow or green tomatoes)
2 fat **garlic cloves**, crushed
450 g (1 lb) **caster sugar**
50 g (1¾ oz) **English mustard powder**
115 g (4 oz) **plain flour**, sieved
25 g (1 oz) **turmeric**
1 teaspoon **ground coriander**
2 teaspoons **salt**

In a large preserving pan, simmer the cauliflower and onions in 1.1 litres (2 pints) of the vinegar for 10 minutes.

Add the other vegetables, garlic and sugar and cook for a further 10 minutes.

Mix the mustard, flour, spices and salt with the remaining vinegar and add to the cooked vegetables, stirring all the time to prevent lumps from forming.

Stir well and simmer for a further 10 minutes.

Spoon into cooled, sterilised jars and seal with vinegar-proof lids. Label and store for 2 weeks before using.

Plum pot

This is a wonderful way to extend the plum season. Try it as a topping for mini pavlovas, served with whipped cream.

Makes about 4 x 450 g (1 lb) jars
Preparation time: 20 minutes + overnight
Cooking time: about 45 minutes

1.3 kg (3 lb) **plums**, stoned and chopped into large pieces
450 g (1 lb) **raisins** or **sultanas**
2 large **oranges** (175–225 g/ 6–8 oz each), sliced and chopped into small pieces
1.3 kg (3 lb) **granulated sugar**
butter (optional)

Put all the fruit and the sugar into a large non-metallic bowl. Cover and leave overnight.

The next day, transfer the mixture to a large preserving pan and heat slowly until the sugar is dissolved, stirring all the time.

Bring to the boil and then simmer until the mixture is fairly thick – about 30 minutes. A knob of butter can be added during cooking to reduce any scum.

Pour into cooled, sterilised jars and then seal and label.

Variations Try this using sultanas with Victoria or greengage plums, and raisins and a dark brown sugar with dark plums. It can also be made using fresh apricots.

Spiced honey orange slices

These make a lovely gift at Christmas time and look particularly attractive when presented with two or three other jars of different preserves.

Makes about 4 x 450 g (1 lb) jars
Preparation time: 30 minutes
Cooking time: 1 hour 20 minutes

6 **oranges**, cut into 5 mm (¼ inch) thick slices
450 ml (15 fl oz) **white wine** or **cider vinegar**
350 g (12 oz) **granulated sugar**
115 g (4 oz) **clear honey**
1 teaspoon **whole cloves**
5 cm (2 inch) **cinnamon stick**
1 tablespoon **coriander seeds**, crushed
whole cloves, for decoration

Place the orange slices in a pan with enough water to cover. Simmer for 45 minutes until the peel of the fruit is tender. Drain and discard the cooking water.

Put the vinegar, sugar, honey and spices in a pan and bring to the boil. Reduce to simmering point and then add the orange slices. Simmer gently for 15–20 minutes until the zest of the fruit becomes translucent.

Strain off and reserve the liquid and carefully pack the slices into cooled, sterilised jars. Place two or three slices around the inside of the jar and then pack the remaining slices down the centre to make them look attractive.

If necessary, return the liquid to the pan and boil rapidly for 5–10 minutes to reduce to a syrup.

Pour the syrup over the oranges, filling to the brim and removing any air bubbles by inserting a knife or wooden skewer to release the bubbles. Place one or two cloves in each jar as it is filled. Seal with vinegar-proof lids and label.

Index